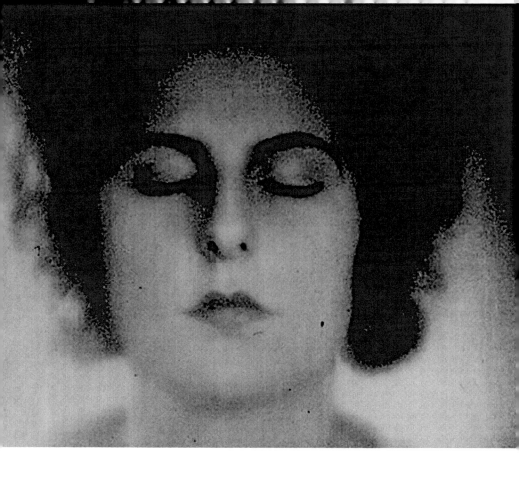

Leni Riefenstahl: "I was never a Nazi. I lived for art and for cinema. And I never hated the Jews. My best friends in the film's industry were Jews, and I always admired their creativity. Everybody knew that, and this infuriated Goebbels, Himmler and the SS."

# LENI RIEFENSTAHL's LAST WORDS ABOUT HITLER,

## GOEBBELS, NAZIS AND THE JEWS.

Date of Publication: August 6, 2014
Published by Times Square Press
http://timessquarepress.com/
Printed in the United States of America and Germany.
The French and German versions, first appeared in November 1979.

Website of the author:
www.maximilliendelafayettebibliography.org/biblio
Contact: Delafayette6@aol.com

Maximillien de Lafayette

This book is based upon Maximillien de Lafayette's book: The Complete Story of the Planned Escape of Hitler: The Nazi-Spain-Argentina Coverup.

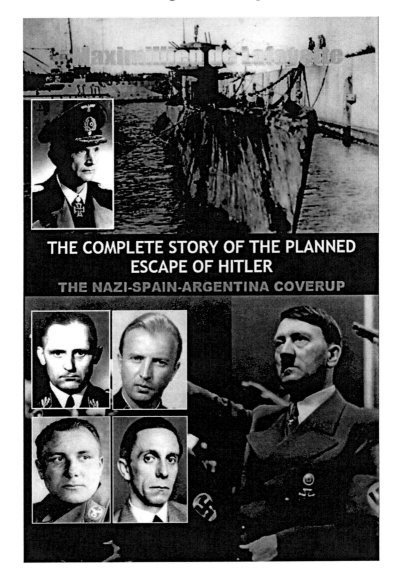

THE COMPLETE STORY OF THE PLANNED ESCAPE OF HITLER
THE NAZI-SPAIN-ARGENTINA COVERUP

# LENI RIEFENSTAHL's LAST WORDS ABOUT HITLER, GOEBBELS, NAZIS AND THE JEWS

Maximillien de Lafayette

Author's website:
www.maximilliendelafayettebibliography.org/biblio

TIMES SQUARE PRESS
http://timessquarepress.com/

New York   Berlin
2014

# Table of Contents

*** *** ***

Leni Riefenstahl with Adolf Hitler.

# My interview with Leni Riefenstahl

In January 1972 in München, I had a long chat with Leni Riefenstahl (Helene Berta Amalie). We spoke about so many things; the Third Reich in general, and Hitler, Eva Braun, Josef Goebbels, his wife Magda and the rumors surrounding the escape of Hitler, and of course her "Triumph des Willens", and her two favorite films "Das Blaue Licht", and "Die weiße Hölle vom Piz Palü" a film she co-directed with G W Pabst.

Leni

A scene from the film "Triumph des Willens" staged and directed by Leni Riefenstahl.

And what she told me was mind-bending. For instance:

a-Hitler had a lot of respect for women.
He thought women were more creative than men on an artistic level. Adolf Hitler admired few people in his life, mostly women...Zarah Leander, he called her the "Divine Zarah", which made Josef Goebbels a little bit jealous...Hitler had a very special affection for Magda Goebbels who thought of her as the "Most perfect German woman", Eva (Eva Braun) of course, Hanna Reitsch, Princess Stephanie Marie von Hohenlohe's (She was Jewish), who gave her so many gifts and a castle...and me (Leni) to a certain degree.

b-Josef Goebbels was not a "pure Aryan"; he was a half-Jew.

c-Hitler himself had something Jewish in him...in his blood, and he created a new family tree to hide that secret that haunted him all his life. His nephew, William Patrick Hitler knew about it and he was constantly blackmailing him.

d-Hitler and Eva did not die in the bunker in Berlin; they escape with Martin Bormann, two days before the Russians entered the bunker. I know that for sure. I don't know all the details, nobody does. (My note: Bormann did not escape with Hitler.)

Leni, the actress.

Hitler with Dr. Josef Goebbels "The Intellectual Clown" as he has been called by Leni Riefenstahl.

The fuhrerbunker

Leni Riefenstahl filming the 1934 Nuremberg Rally. Her 1935 film "Triumph of the Will" was hailed as one of the best propaganda films in modern history.

# A SECRET AIRPLANE CAPABLE OF FLYING 6,000 KILOMETERS NON-STOP.

But from what I heard, during his last stand, Hitler received a message from a mysterious woman to get out of Berlin. The message contained a reference made to a secret airplane capable of flying 6,000 kilometers non-stop. People at the bunker did not take the message very seriously. A second message was delivered to Magda Goebbels. I think it came from Maria Orsic. Magda would not leave her husband. I am absolutely certain that Hitler, Bormann and Kammler escaped aboard what the Americans call a UFO.

Leni Riefenstahl, Director of "Triumph des Willens".

The craft made a short stop in Poland and continued its flight to Argentina. People who where very close to Hitler were saying that Hanna Reitsch flew the craft.

Leni continues her story: Two or three years after the war, I heard a new story about Hitler's escape, totally different from the first one, and it goes like this:
Hitler, Eva, Bormann and Kammler were taken to a secret location on the Baltic Sea where the Luftwaffe and SS were experimenting with a new kind of airplanes...call them UFOs if you want. Two special spacecrafts of a bizarre shape were waiting for them.
One craft crashed in the Baltic Sea, and the other one managed to fly in an unconventional manner.

20

Martin Bormann

Its flight pattern was strange. This very craft took them rapidly to a secret naval base, where they boarded a U-Boat.
More SS officers would later join Hitler.

Hanna Reitsch, then, the world most famous woman pilot, inspecting a German anti-gravity circular craft.
In 1975, Hanna Reitsch stated that Maria Orsic's vision launched Germany's Bell-UFO programs. Hanna Reitsch was unnecessary put on trial. She survived the war and died on August 24, 1979 in Frankfurt, from a heart attack.

Hanna Reitsch

Captain Heinz Schaeffer, Captain of the "U-977".

Dr. Winfried Otto Schumann

23

They did the same thing...they flew aboard one of the "Vrils" which was stationed in the "Alpenfestung"...they fled the base to South America, and Neuschwabenland without leaving any trace. Walter Reinmar told me that Heinz Schaeffer, Captain of the "U-977" (German submarine) which was stationed in the Baltic Sea took Hitler, Eva and Bormann to Argentina.

It took them almost 4 months to reach Argentina. They manage to escape with the help of a very powerful British Lord and the American military high command. From Argentina, they went to a military base in the Antarctic.

After the war, Schaeffer was recruited by the Americans.

Worth mentioning that Heinz Schaeffer was questioned by the Argentinian and American authorities and was released short after."

## Leni: Traudl Junge was in the bunker, but she saw nothing.

-Do you believe what Traudl Junge has said about the suicide of Hitler?

Leni: She is an opportunist and a liar. She saw nothing.

-But she was in the bunker with Hitler.

Leni: She was in the bunker, I know that, but she saw nothing. When the gun-shot was heard, and I don't believe that either, Junge was probably typing something in her room...far from Hitler and Eva's room. She said it herself, "I did not hear a shot, and I did not see the Fuhrer's body." Linge told her that Hitler committed suicide.

Besides how could anybody hear a shot coming from Hitler room when the room is sound-proof? It is impossible.

-You had some sort of a heated discussion with Traudl Junge... (Interrupted)

Leni: She wanted to write her memoirs...a book. She asked me if I could contribute something to the book, some stories or what I have talked about with Hitler and Goebbels.

I told her I am not interested.

*** *** ***

Adolf Hitler awarding Hanna Reitsch the Iron Cross 2nd Class in March 1941.

And one thing led to other thing, and we ended shouting at each other. I think yes you could call it a heated talk, but she started it, not me. You see I don't want to be part of any of this. I rather focus on what I am going to do next...in my life.

-Like what for instance?

Leni: Documentaries, may be a series of a few photo-albums, something like that. Let me tell you something. No one, nobody who is still alive will ever dare to tell the truth. Some tried and were killed. I can assure you that almost 90% of what it has been said about the war is either grossly fabricated or false. After all, who writes history books? The winners, the victorious, not the losers, not the defeated.

Leni: Did you talk to her?

-I did.

Leni: So what do you think?

-Think about what?

Leni: Traudl Junge.

-I don't know Leni. It is too early. So 90% is false! Hitler's suicide was staged. Stories about Hitler and especially his psychological profile is nonsense, as you have once said. Do you mean what was said about Hitler, and his cruelty was not true?

Leni: You are putting words in my mouth.

Eva Braun with Adolf Hitler at his retreat in in the Bavarian Alps.

Leni Riefenstahl with Adolf Hitler on the set of her film "Triumph des Willens" staged and directed by Leni Riefenstahl.

---

**I have never never never denied the hideous acts and crimes committed by Hitler.**

I was talking about his escape, and what Hanna Reitsch has told me. And everybody now is misquoting me. Lot of untrue things were said about Hitler, basically stupid stories fabricated by the Americans.

They said he was homosexual, he was not. They said he attracted venereal disease from a Jewish prostitute, he did not. They said he poisoned Blondi, his dog, he didn't; Hitler and Eva Braun took Blondi on the U-Boat that landed on a shore in Argentina.

He did not kill his dog. Hitler did not poison Blondi. He adored Blondi. It never happened. No reason to.

Why should he poison his dog? He loved Blondi.

Hitler with his dog Blondi.

---

Goebbels did not like dogs. One day Hitler and Goebbels had an argument about Blondi. Let me see was it Goebbels or Himmler? No, no, it was Goebbels.

Goebbels said to Hitler: "What do you get out of this dog?"

You see Goebbels always asked inquisitive questions like this.

And Hitler answered: From Eva, I get understanding. From you, support, and from Blondi, loyalty..."

-How did you know about this?

Leni: Dr. Morell...He told me lots of things, he was always there.

Leni continued...They said he was a bad painter, he was not. Yes he was not great at portraiture but good enough in landscape.

They said he ate meat and his vegetarian diet was a bluff. Not true, he was vegetarian. They said he did not finish his formal schooling and did not read.

It is not true, he was a vivid reader. He read Nietzsche, translated verses from the poetry of Victor Hugo and Shakespeare. He read Latin and Greek classics in German of course. The American said that he didn't take women seriously and had no respect for women. Not True. He was a perfect gentleman with women.
He always kissed their hands, spoke softly with them, and even exchanged jokes with them. So on...and all these stories were coming from supposedly educated Americans and well informed spies and intelligence agents.
If the American government was either misled or intended on spreading false information about Hitler, then I am not surprised at all that they didn't know a thing about his escape and the remaining years he spent in Argentina.
I must admit, few in America knew about Hitler's escape, most certainly generals who were from the high military hierarchy, but they kept their mouths shut...they were desperate to acquire German technology.

Leni Riefenstahl

The legendary U Boat 977.

The U 977 when it reached Argentina after approximately 120 days a sea; a world record for a submarine!

## Leni: The Americans needed German scientists, Nazi or not Nazi.

The Americans needed German scientists, Nazi or not Nazi to develop new kind of military weapons systems and surpass the Russian military capabilities.

-Still, he was a brutal mass killer. Right?

Leni: Many were. How about the carpet bombings of German cities, Dresden, Düsseldorf, Berlin?

Who did the bombings and killed 11 million Germans, mostly women, children and old people? Who? The Americans and the British. War can't be justified. And in my opinion any person who is part of any war justified or not is a beast! Yes, Hitler was not an angel. He killed millions of people...Brilliant in a way, but he lost his mind and by the end could not function properly. I am absolutely sure that he was under the influence of two maniacs, Bormann and Goebbels. I never like them.

They were evil, something else I should tell you, Hitler was constantly drugged by his personal physician, Dr. Morell who was part of the Bormann-Goebbels conspiracy.

-So you are absolutely convinced that Hitler did escape and spent his last days in Argentina?

Leni: Yes I do.

-I am a little bit confused here. You just said Hitler escaped on a U-Boat. Earlier you said Hanna Reitsch flew him to Argentina on one of those Maria Orsic's flying machines.

(Interrupted)

Leni: Oh no! I never said that. What I said was what Reitsch told me. It was her story, not mine.

-So which one is the right story? Which version?

Leni: I don't know and I don't care.

Why are you so much interested in Hitler's escape?

-Weren't you at some point interested too?

Leni: Years and years ago...I don't want to revisit the past. I am still suffering from it. Did you know for a few months I was hungry...I had no food...and for a very long time I was penniless and unemployed. Nobody would hire me. Nobody cared about me. I starved. So why should I care about Hitler or be interested in his escape? I had enough!

31

-Can I ask you a few questions about Josef Goebbels?
Leni: Goebbels! A pervert. He slept with all those little stupid aspiring actresses. You should ask Zara (Zara Leander) and she will tell you everything. Poor Magda! Goebbels? What a hideous person! Evil! He created Hitler. He gave me so much troubles. Himmler and Josef Goebbels were the devil incarnated.

Leni in her early career as an actress.

One worse than the other. Hitler never liked academicians; you know the university's professor type.

## Hitler never trusted intellectuals.

Hitler never trusted intellectuals. And here we have, Goebbels, a doctor in literature who spoke many languages.
A pure intellectual, yet, they were close friends and associates in crime. Try to figure it out. I couldn't!
And let me tell you something else...back then, we heard lots of stories about Goebbels being a half Jew. Oh Yes! Believe me. Did you know some of Hitler's best friends and most admired and trusted people were Jews?
-Common! Really? Who?
Leni: First, let's start with Princess Stephanie Marie von Hohenlohe. She was Jewish. And even though she was Jewish, Adolf Hitler overlooked her ethnic background.

Princess Stephanie with Fritz Wiedemann in 1941.

Left: Fritz Wiedemann.

In 1938, Adolph Hitler gave Stephanie the Leopoldskron Castle, which he confiscated from Max Reinhardt, director of a German theater, and on the top of that, he gave her a most unusual title "Honorary Aryan", and the insignia of the NAZI party, even though she was Jewish! How can you explain that to me?

Here is a brief excerpt from an article published about this woman by Life Magazine, June 26, 1939 issue:
"He (Wiedemann, the German Consul in San Francisco,) and Hitler are thinking of summoning Stephanie, Princess Hohenlohe to San Francisco. This remarkable woman, with her wide international contacts, has more than once performed miracles for the Third Reich... She can give parties to which her title will attract the potentates of the West Coast, and 'Captain Fritz' will casually drop in.

Stephanie Marie von Hohenlohe, one of Adolf Hitler's most distinguished spies, and an international celebrity with strong contacts in Europe and the United States, was captured by the OSS, and later detained in a German detention camp in Texas.

When she arrived to San Francisco in December 1939, the FBI began to watch her around the clock. J. Edgar Hoover put her under 24 hour surveillance, because he was fully convinced that Hitler has sent her to San Francisco to help Fritz Wiedemann set up a Nazi espionage network. Hoover called her the "Most dangerous woman in the world." And finally the FBI arrested her in December 1941.

Princess Stephanie Marie von Hohenlohe knew a lot about Germany's exotic weapons and anti-gravity flying machines, and the Nazi secret base in the Baltic Sea.

What she told the OSS and the FBI about Maria Orsic and the various types and mode of operation of those anti-gravity flying machines was mind-bending.

Leopoldskron Castle in Salzburg, Austria, a gift from Hitler to the Jewish Princess Stephanie Marie von Hohenlohe.

Left: The Princess on the cover of the excellent book "Hitler's Spionin" by Martha Schad.

---

But she was polite and very proper, but not so, when she was asked by the FBI to draw a psychological profile of Adolf Hitler. Later on, she became a spy for the OSS, the precursor of the CIA.

35

Leni Riefenstahl

# Many of Hitler and Goering's friends were Jews.

-OK Leni, who else?

Leni: Zarah, Zarah Leander. He was crazy about her. He called her the greatest actress and singer in Europe and nicknamed her "Diva"; the Diva of the Third Reich. She was Jewish.

He knew that, and she told him herself.

You know Zarah is not a "Pure Aryan", as many times Goebbels pointed out. He disliked her a lot.

Let me tell you this little funny story. In a reception after one of her recitals, Josef Goebbels began to chat with Zarah, and as usual he was surrounded by his thugs and bodyguards.

So Goebbels congratulated Zarah, smiled sarcastically and said to her: Zarah...a Jewish name, isn't it? Interesting!

And Zarah (With the speed of light) replied: Josef...a Jewish name, isn't it? Interesting!

Zarah Leander was sharp.

Leni: Very sharp.

Left: Hugo Gutmann.

Hitler was not a flamboyant man. He did not like fashion, military medals and decorations. He used to make jokes about Goering's outfits, his white coat, and wardrobe.

If you look at Hitler's photos, you will see he is wearing one medal, only one...the Iron Cross. He earned it for bravery during the Great War (World War I); it was a second class Iron Cross. Then, he was recommended for first class Iron Cross.

And who recommended him? Gutman! Hugo Gutmann, was a Jew.

He was a Jewish officer in the German army...he was Hitler's boss (Commandant). Hitler remained grateful to Gutman for the rest of his life. He always spoke about Gutmann with lots of respected and gratitude.

-OK, who else?

Leni: Erhard Milch. He was Hermann Goering's right hand and a close friend. Milch was a General. Goering made him a State Secretary, and he put him on the Luftwaffe high command board. Goering made him. Then, Goering found out he was a Jew. His mother was Jewish. Goering did not want to lose Milch. Erhard Milch was very important to him.

But Goering feared that the Gestapo might find out. Do you know what he did? I will tell you. Goering forced his mother to sign a statement signed before a notary that Erhard Milch is not her son.

Erhard Milch was Jewish and a close friend of Goering. Appointed Air Inspector General of the Luftwaffe during the Nazi invasion of Europe, by Hermann Goering.

Field Marshal Erhard Milch on the cover of Time Magazine.

\*\*\*   \*\*\*   \*\*\*

**Leni: All politicians and heads of state are hypocrites.**

-So was Hitler a hypocrite?
Leni: All politicians and heads of state are hypocrites.
Even the Pope! Don't let me start with the Pope, please!
-Did the Vatican help Nazis, SS people, and war criminals escape from Germany?
Leni: Yes. Absolutely.
-The Pope himself?
Leni: The Pope? No. Cardinals and bishops...yes!
-Hitler and Dr. Goebbels were well connected to the Vatican. And had many cardinals, bishops and priests as friends in the Vatican and Germany. Correct?
Leni: Not many friends, no. But thanks to the cunning genius of Goebbels, Hitler and Himmler established strong relations with some of the most important figures in the Vatican. Goebbels was a close friend to the very powerful Cardinal Cesare Orsenigo, the envoy or representative of the Pope in Germany.

Cardinal Cesare Orsenigo (left) with Dr. Josef Goebbels in Berlin.

Germany and the Vatican signing the Reichskonkordat on 20
July October 1933.
From left to right: German Vice-Chancellor Franz von Papen,
official representative of Germany, Cardinal Giuseppe
Pizzardo, Pope Pius XII (Then, Cardinal Pacelli), and to the far
right, Rudolf Buttmann, ambassador of Germany.

Goebbels in a reception at his honor in the Vatican, Rome.

Pope Pius XII (Then, Cardinal Pacelli), leaving the presidential palace in Germany in March 1929.

Vatican's priests and bishops saluting *a la Hitler*.

Leni Riefenstahl with Josef Goebbels at the Berlin Olympics.

**Leni: Germany needed the Vatican and vice versa. Everything started with the Reichskonkordat.**

-Did any of those cardinals and bishops help Hitler escape?
Leni: I don't think so. Very few knew about Hitler's escape.
-Who for example?
Leni: Eva (Eva Braun) of course, Goebbels, Martin Borman...he was the mastermind behind Hitler's escape, who else? Who else? I assume Eva's sister, and of course her husband.
I don't think either Geoving or Himmler knew....Who else?
Admiral Karl Doenitz for sure! Hitler needed U-Boats to escape. I don't think Josef Goebbels told his wife Magda. This woman was a terrific lady, and did you know her nurse was Jewish!!! Any way why are you interviewing me?
Are you working on a book? Is this why you wanted to see me?
You know that friend of yours who worked at Il Tempo...no sorry at La Coriera del Sera interviewed me too, but she vanished.
When I called the newspaper, they told me that she is no longer there, she does not work for them anymore.

Leni, the actress.

And guess what? I heard that she was threatened, her life was in danger, and...she disappeared! Totally! Completely!

-Did Hitler use a double?

Leni: Sure he did.

-How did you know that?

Leni: How did I know that?

Of course I knew. Goebbels ...Oh dear, Goebbels again...any way, being a well-known cinema director in Germany and Hitler's favorite director, and because I worked with Goebbels on two or three documentaries and a few films, and because I knew a lot about maquillage (Make-up), Goebbels asked me about the best ways or "techniques" to disguise a person, or make him look like somebody else.

**Leni: Goebbels knew exactly what kind of films Hitler liked and disliked.**

He started to ask me a few questions like, if I liked American films, Hollywood's movies, if I liked Clark Gable for instance, and other actresses...questions like that. Hitler was a cinema buff. He loved Hollywood's film, and Goebbels creates a large cinematech for him. Goebbels knew exactly what kind of films Hitler liked and disliked.

Hitler loved cartoons, he loved Mickey Mouse. Goebbels gave him a dozen of Mickey Mouse films as a Christmas present.

Goebbels created a special department on American films which were considered to be either pro-Jewish or anti Jewish. He asked me to help him in selecting some of those films and I refused.

I told him I am a filmmaker and not a film historian.

Then he asked me if I would go to America and meet with cinema directors in Hollywood and find out what kind of films they were making about Hitler and Germany. And I said no.

Finally, Georg Gyssling (Germany's Consul in Los Angeles) was chosen to do that. Gyssling would choose American films and send them to Goebbels.

You know, Goebbels was in charge of German cinema during the Third Reich and he knew lots of actresses, but he did not show any interest in men actors...and one question will lead to another question. He also asked me about what was special about Hitler's face? Did I like his mustaches?

Did I like his facial expressions? Was Adolf Hitler over acting or seems to act dramatically while delivering his speeches?

Georg Gyssling, Germany's Consul in Los Angeles with Leni
Riefenstahl.

And finally he asked me if with my cinema techniques I can duplicate his face, meaning using cinema maquillage (make-up) on somebody to make him look like Hitler?

I was very surprised to hear this kind of questions, and especially when he asked me whether I could make a person look like Adolf Hitler!

Very candidly, I asked him if he was planning on producing a special documentary on Adolf Hitler, or was he thinking about presenting a stage play, in which a person should look like Adolf Hitler. And he said yes. And I believed him.

Then he asked him if among the extras I used in my films, if there is a person who could act very well and look like Hitler...to a certain degree? I said no. Then he asked if I knew any actress who looked like Eva Braun?

And I said no.

But without thinking or having any suspicions I said to him, Eva Braun's face is not difficult to duplicate. With a professional cinema or stage maquillage (make-up) I can make an actress look like Eva Braun. He smiled and said excellent.

I asked him who is writing the scenario (The script) and the play, and he replied: "Me! I want to surprise the Fuhrer. It is going to be a good surprise. Don't tell anybody. It is a secret.

You promise?"

And I replied of course. Before leaving, I asked if I could read the script, in case if he is considering me to be the director of the film.

And he replied, "I will let you know. But remember, it is a secret. Do not spoil the surprise." He never called me again.

And I totally forgot about the whole thing, until I was arrested and interrogated by the Americans and was asked during hideous and never-ending interrogatories whether Hitler used a double or not.

And suddenly something back-flashed in my head! Something hit me. And I knew what it was!!! And in seconds, I remembered all the questions Goebbels have asked me...just like that....and especially his questions about face maquillage, and how to make a person look like Adolf Hitler. I will never forget that moment.

The military interrogator asked me again, "Did Adolf Hitler use a double?" I think they repeated the same question twice or three times. But I was somewhere else.

Then he shouted at me: "ANSWER THE QUESTION!!" And I replied, "I don't know." A tall strong man with short hair a la brosse, who looked like a savage wrestler approached me and said loudly, "You better tell us the truth!"
And I said with a very low voice, "I am not sure, I haven't seen a double of Hitler." He screamed and said, "What do you mean you are not sure?" And I replied, "I told you the truth. I am not sure. I don't know!"
It was a nightmare. Questions after questions after questions, non-stop! I think I fainted.
-And now after all these years, and what you have heard and read about Hitler's double or doubles, have you changed your mind?
Leni: Yes. I am sure now. Adolf Hitler used a double.
-Leni, please look at these two picture (Below). Tell me, is this man Adolf Hitler or his double?

Leni (After looking at the photograph for less than five seconds) said: This is NOT Adolf Hitler!!

The double of Adolf Hitler decorates members of Hitler's Nazi youth organization "Hitler Jugend" outside the Chancellery Bunker in Berlin, on April 25, 1945.

---

-A double then?

Leni: Yes! Definitely a double.....Oh my God... he looks exactly like him...but I can tell...he is not Adolf Hitler...

-How can you tell?

Leni: First, the ears...these are not the ears of Adolf Hitler.

Second, the smile, this is not the smile of Hitler...The upper lip...no...no...this is not Adolf Hitler. A very good replica...a very convincing double!

I took more than 3,000 shots of Adolf Hitler from all angles. I know very well the face of Adolf Hitler. Wait a minute...wait a minute, I saw this picture in a newsreel.

I remember now...it is really amazing.

-And how about this photograph (Below), Leni?

Is this man Adolf Hitler?

Leni: No! His double! I know every inch of the face of Hitler.

I coached him for my film "Triumph des Willens".

I directed him, and I created and shot special scenes to fit the dramatic expressions of his face. And I can tell you, this man in this photograph is not Adolf Hitler. This man is the double of Hitler.
-And this man (Below) in photo A and B, is he Adolf Hitler?
Leni: Another double.

Photo 1: Another picture of Hitler's double.

Photo 2
Another picture of Hitler's double.

-Are you telling me you never knew that Hitler had a double or suspected anything about that?
Leni: I did not know. But I suspected something.
I don't think anybody knew back then, except of course Goebbels, Muller (General Muller) and Bormann, and the maquillage artist. Is this man (Pointing the photo) still alive.

The last photo taken of Hitler's double in 1945.

---

-He was shot in the head...Murdered. Assassinated!
Leni: Who shot him in the head?
-We don't know. No witnesses. But many are pointing the finger at Martin Bormann.
Leni: "I know every inch of the face of Hitler. And I can tell you this man in this photograph is not Adolf Hitler. This man is the double of Hitler."
Leni: Are you writing a book on the Third Reich?

-No, I am not working on a book. But perhaps I might... one of those days...years from now.

Leni: Be careful. Don't ever dare to say anything positive about Adolf Hitler...no more comments.

-Why should I say anything good about Adolf Hitler? Some of my parents were killed by the SS!!

Leni: And if you decide to write a book and publish it soon, I want to read everything you wrote about me before you print the book. Do you understand? I want to read and approve each word you wrote, please. Tell the truth. Don't exaggerate. Don't dramatize things. And don't misquote me and don't say lies. I am not Max Schmelling but I will punch you in the face as hard as I can (Smiling).

## HITLER's 4 BIGGEST MISTAKES

-Hitler made many mistakes. In your opinion, which ones were his biggest mistakes?

Leni: Hitler made four big, very big mistakes.

The first and the biggest one as everybody knows was the Jewish Holocaust. Few knew about the mass killing of the Jews. Most certainly I did not know a thing about these atrocities. Hitler never spoke to me about the Jews.

The second big mistake was his stubbornness; he never listened to his generals, he was an imposing civic leader but a lousy military strategist.

The third big mistake is of course...when he declared war on America. And the fourth big one, when he attacked Russia.

-He never said a word to you about the Jews?

Leni: Never!

-I know you are not anti-Semitic....

(Interrupting). Leni: Listen Maximillien, I want you and the whole world to know that some of my best friends were Jewish.

And those who I deeply admired in the cinema business and loved to work with on the set of my films were Jews. Art has no religion, and cinema is universal; it embraces everything, except racism. None of my films were anti-Semitic! I worked and lived for cinema, and my artistic expression, not for Hitler, not for the Nazi Party, and not for politics.

54

And this is how we ended our chat.
We hugged each other and I left. And I knew I will never have another chance to talk to Leni Riefenstahl. I felt I will never see her again. Was this exceptional woman unfairly treated by the media and her accusers? Did she tell the truth, the whole truth? I don't know. Probably I will never know.
But when Leni's eyes were soaked in tears, and leaned toward me and said, "I have been victimized...I made lots of mistakes in my life, but I was never a Nazi, I never joined the party....I lived only for my art." When she said that, I knew she was telling the truth. And I believed her. Leni Riefenstahl died in Berlin in 2003, at the age of 101.

*** *** ***

# ABOUT LENI RIEFENSTAHL

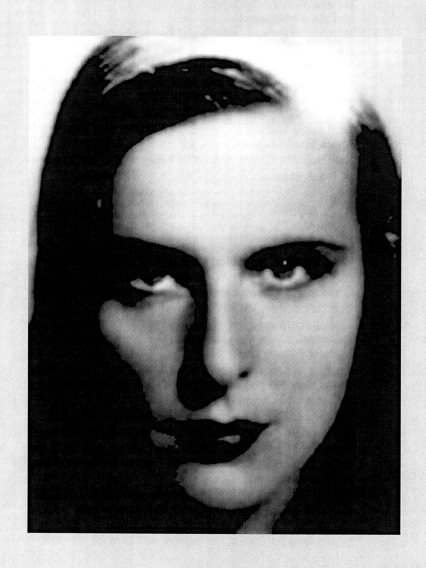

**Some Facts and for the Record:**

- In 1946, the International Olympic Committee awarded Leni a gold medal for her film "Olympia."
- After World War Two, Leni was imprisoned by the allies because of her artistic contributions to the Nazis (Films and documentaries).
- In 1948, a German court found Leni to be "not a Nazi."
- Again, in 1952, a second German court cleared her from all accusations and charges, and especially from any collaboration, and/or any contribution which could be considered by the court as war crimes.
- Leni was never a member of the Nazi party.
- Leni knew absolutely nothing of Hitler and Himmler's "Jews Final Solution."
- Leni was absolutely cleared of being a Nazi collaborator by the Americans, British, French, and Russians.

*** *** ***

## Leni's Quotes:

- Yes I admired Hitler for what did for Germany when he came to power. Everybody did. And yes, I did a lot for Germany as an artist and a filmmaker not as a politician, or an ideologist, and Hitler new that.
- I was never a member of the Nazi party, never ever. I was an outsider. Anyway, Himmler, Goebbels and the Nazi's hierarchy never trusted me.
- On two occasions, the SS tried to kill me. I told Hitler about that. He became very upset and promised me that no harm will come to me.
- Millions of German women adored Hitler. I did not.
- No I didn't see my films as a propaganda. I just made beautiful artistic films. I didn't care about politics, I was never interested in politics, and I never understood how politics work.
- I never had any political reasons for making these films (German propaganda films and documentaries).
- No no no, I did not make films for Hitler or Nazism. I made films for myself, for my art, and love for cinema.

Leni Riefenstahl

Leni in her early career as an aspiring actress.

- Of all the things I have done in my life as an artist, dance made me the happiest and fascinated me the most.
- I was only interested in how I could make a film that was not stupid like a newsreel, but more interesting.
- Himmler said that I was half Jewish. Ridiculous. I am not Jewish. Himmler said that to Hitler, but of course Hitler did not believe him.
- From an interview with the BBC: I am one of millions who thought Hitler had all the answers. We saw only the good things, we didn't know bad things were to come", she told BBC News.
- From an interview with Hoffman: I experienced Hitler for the first time in 1932 in the Berlin Sports Palace. It was also the first political meeting that I ever went to. I was amazed to see the tremendous hypnotic power Hitler exercised over his audience, like a hypnotist who charmed everyone and held them spellbound. It was uncanny and the spark jumped over to me too.
- Josef Goebbels was worse than Adolf Hitler.
- Himmler and Josef Goebbels were the devil incarnated.

---

# FROM THE ALBUM

Admiral Karl Doenitz with Hitler in Hitler's bunker in 1945.

Hitler's bunker after it was demolished in 1947.

The Reichstag after its capture by the Red Army on June 3,
1945.

---

Hitler's apartment.

The building housing Hitler's apartment at No. 16,
Prinzregentenstrasse.

From L to R: Maria Orsic, circa 1940. Traudl Junge in 2002.
In 2002, Mrs. Junge told me: "We did receive a message from Maria Orsic, and it was delivered to Mrs. Goebbels by Inge Schulz... Bormann read it first..."

---

From left to right: Magda Goebbels, Adolf Hitler, Minister of propaganda, Dr. Josef Goebbels, and three of their children in the Bavarian Alps.

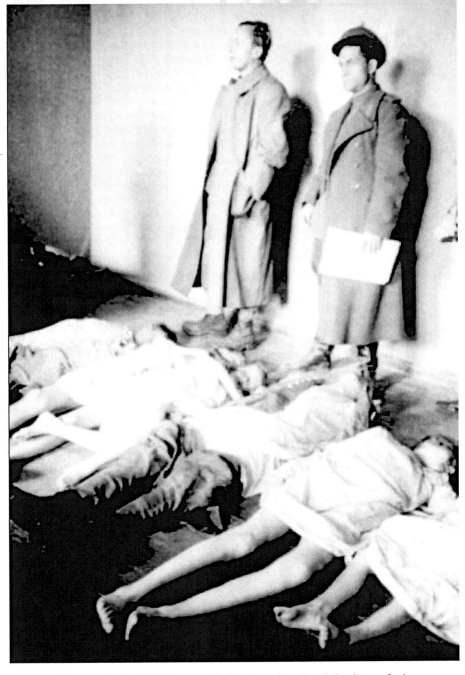

Soldiers of the Red Army displaying the dead bodies of the daughters of Josef Goebbels, poisoned by Dr. Helmut Kunz. Maria Orsic tried to prevent this unnecessary tragedy from happening, but nobody would listen to her. The once upon a time a respected and trusted medium, Maria Orsic became a persona non-grata in the eyes of Himmler and his henchmen.

Marshal Georgy Konstantinovich Zhukov and Russian officers
looking at the charred bodies of Josef Goebbels, his wife Magda
and their children who were poisoned in Hitler's bunker.
Below: The charred body of Josef Goebbels

The canisters of gasoline that were allegedly used to burn the bodies of the Goebbels and "fabricated" doubles of Hitler and Eva Braun, which were never found.

Russian soldiers carrying two dead bodies in a re-enactment
scene of the suicide of Hitler and Eva Braun.

Eva Braun with her brother-in-law Hermann Fegelein during his wedding ceremony in 1944. Fegelin married Gretl Braun, Eva's sister).

Hans Baur with Hitler.

Hitler's personal pilot, Hans Baur told his Russian interrogators: "Adolf Hitler, Eva Braun and General Hermann Fegelein escaped aboard a Ju 52."

## 1-The mastermind of Hitler's escape:

Martin Bormann

Josef Goebbels

Hermann Fegelein

Heinrich Muller

Admiral Karl Doenitz

283

Leni on the set of a film.

Leni

# ADDENDUM

Traudl Junge with Nazi officers in Berlin. Far right: Erich
Kempka.
Nee Gertraud Humps, March 16, 1920-February 10, 2002,
Traudle Junge was the private secretary of Adolf Hitler from
November 1942 to April 1945).

In the presence of an old friend of mine who worked as a
reporter for Corriere della Sera, and who had a privileged access
to the Vatican, I asked Traudl Junge the following questions:
-Is it true, you typed the last dictated will of Adolf Hitler?
Junge: Yes I did.
-Was Hitler in a good state of mind when he dictated to you his
last will?

Junge: Not totally, I mean he was very emotional, but perfectly alert.
Perhaps not as articulate as he used to be. But he knew perfectly what he was talking about. He had every thing written down on 2 pieces of paper. He dictated...and I typed everything he said.

## Junge: Hitler was always spontaneous and fast.

-Didn't you find something odd about this?
Junge: What do you mean? I don't understand.
-You just told me that he was dictating to you from an already written document...two papers you said. Did he ever before dictate anything to you from something he already wrote down? Perhaps, some sort of a prepared statement for instance.
Junge (Pausing and thinking): No.
You are right. No he didn't.
He was always spontaneous and fast, nothing was pre-prepared, or written down. He didn't need to.
-So why this time he did it differently?
Junge: Because it was an exceptionally important document. It was his last will. Don't you think so?
-I do. I understand. Did you notice something unusual about him while dictating his last will?
Junge: He was a little bit confused, and he was reading very slowly. No, I should not say confused...he was rather tired and he seemed to me as if he was reading something he did not put all his thoughts and brilliant mind in it...he was reading the papers with some difficulty. You have to understand every body in the bunker was in state of fear and shock.
-Didn't Josef Goebbels interrupt Adolf Hitler while he was dictating to you, every time Hitler seemed to read the pre-written pages with some difficulty?
Junge: Yes. Once or twice.
-Did Josef Goebbels ever interrupt Hitler before?
Junge: Nobody did. Nobody would dare.
-So how come Goebbels did this time?
Junge: I don't know.
-Was Martin Bormann present in the room when Hitler was dictating to you?
Junge: Yes.
-Did he make any comment? Did he say anything to you?
Junge: No, but he did add some remarks...notes...

-Does Hitler usually dictate to you from written notes?
Junge: No. He never did. He hated notes.
-Didn't you find it odd that he was dictating to you his will from notes?
Junge: Yes and no.
-How could you work for a man who murdered millions of people, and I am not talking only about Jews, and...
Junge (Interrupting): Adolf Hitler never talked to me about Jews. It was none of my business. I was simply a secretary.
-But you did know about his mass slaughters?
Junge: Only after the war. And believe me I felt so guilty even though I was not part of it.

**From what she said about Hitler's gun shot:**

"While playing with the Goebbels children on 30 April, suddenly there is the sound of a shot, so loud, so close, that we all fall silent. It echoes on through all the rooms. 'That was a direct hit,' cried Helmut with no idea how right he is.
The Führer is dead now."

\*\*\* \*\*\* \*\*\*

Zarah Leander

## My interview with Zarah Leander, the Diva of the Third Reich.

Q: Many still ask how come you survived the Holocaust, being a Jewish woman?
Zarah: My grandparents were. I never practiced any religion.
Q: Is it because you were Hitler's favorite star?
Zarah: This too.
Q: How did Hitler know about you? I assume from your movies, being the greatest star of German cinema?
Zarah: Before that. He saw some of my stage performances in Vienna.
Q: Is it true that your enormous success was catapulted by the Nazis and especially because Hitler was very fond of you?
Goebbels did mention this on many occasions.

Zarah: I did not only perform for the Nazis.
I was an artist who performed for people from All Europe.
And Goebbels had nothing to do with my success and fame.
In fact, he was jealous of all the successful stars, artists and filmakers in Germany, including Leni Riefenstahl.
Q: But Goebbels financed many of your movies.
Zarah: Untrue. In fact he did not like me at all, because I was not German. He gave me hard time.
Q: Then Hitler interfered and put him in his place, right?
Hitler called you the Diva of the Third Reich.
Zarah: You can say that.
Q: Hilter was your ultimate hero, correct?
Zarah: At the beginning, at the very beginning, yes.
Q: How did you feel when you heard about his suicide?
Zarah: Suicide? No...no... he was not a coward.
Q: What do you mean?

Hitler with Franco.

## Zarah Leander: Hitler did not commit suicide.

Zarah: He did not commit suicide. I can assure that.
Q: He escaped?
(Interrupted)
Zarah: I would not say "escaped"...he had to do what he had to do...he had to leave Germany because he knew what the Russians would do to him if they caught him.
Q: Where did he go?
Zarah: I am not sure.
Q: Any idea?
Zarah: I don't know...I heard lots of stories.
Q: Like what?
Zarah: Well, some have said that Franco helped him...I mean he offered him hospitality after he left Germany. And of course Peron and his wife Eva were also very helpful.
Q: How did he get out of Germany?

Zarah Leander with Josef Goebbels (Left).

Zarah: Again...I am not sure. I heard that Martin Borman and Hanna Reitsch had something to do with it.
Q: What was the role of Hanna Reitsch?
How did she help Hitler?
Zarah: She was a pilot you know, a very experienced and famous pilot, and a test-pilot too. I heard that she flew him to a secret base near Sweden or Denmark...
I don't know the precise location, but somewhere in the Baltic Sea.
Q: And...
Zarah: And...Hitler flew to Spain.
Q: With Hanna Reitsch?
Zarah: No.
Q: So Hitler survived?
Zarah: Apparently.
Q: What else do you know?

84

Zarah: That's all...nothing else.

Q: Have you ever talked to Leni Riefenstahl or Hanna Reitsch about Hitler's escape?

Zarah: No.

Q: Does Leni Riefenstahl know what you know?

Zarah: Ask her...

*** *** ***

## My interview with Simone Signoret
## (Former member of the French Resistance)

**Simone Signoret: Hitler had at least 5 doubles...Germans and one Austrian.**

In 1975, I had a chat with Simone Signoret about Hitler's double and his escape to Argentina.
Here is part of what we talked about.
-Did you know Hitler had a double?
-He had many doubles.
-German doubles?
-At least 5 Germans and one Austrian.
-How did you know?
-People in the cinema and entertainment business talked about it...of course secretly.
-Why secretly?

German soldiers flirting with French women near le Moulin Rouge, where some of France's greatest stars entertained the Nazis.

### Signoret: Goebbels trained at least 4 doubles for Hitler and two women as doubles for Eva Braun.

-Well...because they were still performing in boites (Cabarets, nightclubs) in Paris - and some we thought were collaborators - So they could not talk about it openly because they didn't want to be arrested by the Gestapo or lose their jobs.
-You mean people like Charles Trenet?
-No no no...I can't name names...you understand.
-So entertainers and singers talked about Hitler's doubles.
-Yes...they surely did. Besides, a few artists from Germany who briefly performed in Paris knew about it, and I talked to some of them. Sometimes they denied it, and some other times they would say yes. I remember one German actress who told me that Goebbles trained at least 4 doubles for Hitler and two women as doubles for Eva Braun.
-Do you know their names?
-You mean the women?

-Women and men.
-Women...no. But there is one, I think...she was a new ingénue
and Goebbels' mistress...originally from Baden Baden. She got
the gig. Little did she know that one day she will be drugged and
killed by Goebbles' people.
-Did she?
-What do you mean?
-Was she drugged and killed?
-Yes.
-And Hitler's doubles, did you know who were those doubles?
-By name? No.
But I knew about them from La Resistance (French Resistance)
and our agents in Poland.
-That's right, you had strong connection there.
-Not really. My parents were Jewish. My father was from Poland,
and my mother from Austria. I took my mother's name because I
did not want the Gestapo to know about my Jewish background.
-You did join the resistance after all.
-Yes I did. This is how I knew about Hitler's double.
-How did the resistance know about Hitler's double.
-Well...from some Germans who worked in Paris, and mainly
from Henri Dericourt. You should talk about this to Jean Gabin...
-Henri Dericourt was a double agent, maybe a triple agent. He
worked for the resistance, for the British and the Nazis...he was
associated with Karl Baumelburg, the head of counter sabotage
in France, right?
-There are lots of talks and rumours about Dericourt.
Who knows?

-Dericourt was arrested in France in November
1946.
-Yes, but he was acquitted.
-There is also Georges Pichard who knew about
Hitler's double. You should talk to Jean Gabin.

Left: Henri Dericourt

-Did the French resistance kill Dericourt?
-I can't answer this question. I don't know.
I heard that his pairplane crashed in Laos in
1962 and he died.
-How about Hitler's escape? Did he escape to
Argentina?

89

-Israel secret service believes so.
They are sure he escaped to Argentina. They even tried to kidnap him, but unfortunately they could not get to him. Hitler was well protected and kept on moving from one place to another.
-You reported directly to Charles de Gaulle...
-Sometimes.
-What did Charles de Gaulle think about the possibility of Hitler's escape?
-He didn't say much.
But on one occasion, he let me know that Hitler was still alive.

*** *** ***

## On Hitler's Doubles and Leaders' Doubles.

Of course, Hitler had doubles. This is not inconceivable, for Stalin too had a double known to insiders as Rashid (Rash), real name: Felix Dadaev, who was trained by the Russian actor Alexei Dikkiy at the KGB's headquaters in Moscow.

Left: The real Stalin. Right: Felix Dadaev, Stalin's double.

British soldier Meyrick Edward Clifton James on numerous occasions impersonated Montgomery.
In 1954, Clifton James wrote a book under the title "I Was Monthy's Double", and was published in the United States as "The Counterfeit General Montgomery". And Monty had also a second double called Keith Deamer Banwell.

*** *** ***

Left: The real Montgomery. Right: Meyrick Edward Clifton
James, Monty's double.

Prime Minister Winston Churchill had his own political decoy; a
double, actor Norman Shelley.

Heinrich Himmler used a double to fake his suicide.

Numerous British intelligence agents and spies in Berlin, Munich
and Switzerland knew very well that Himmler did not commit
suicide.

Joe Reeder, the under-secretary for the United Stated Army
(1993-1997), said many worlds' leaders have used a double, and
he named names: Joseph Stalin, Fidel Castro, George W. Bush
and Osama bin Laden.

Using a double was not a novelty, or something unusual.

On April 19, 1945, the New York Times wrote, "He (The double)
was supposed to be a total look-alike, and he was trained to be
Hitler and was supposedly going to die a martyr's death..."

A top secret military report based upon military interrogations
proved beyond the shadow of a doubt that "Martin Borman has
selected at least one double for Adolf Hitler, and Minister of
Propaganda of the Third Reich, Josef Goebbels has personally
trained six doubles to impersonate Adolf Hitler."

*** *** ***

92

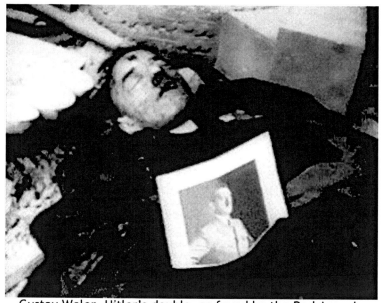

Gustav Weler, Hitler's double, as found by the Red Army in Berlin.

A Russian soldier photographing the dead body of Gustav Weler, Hitler's double.

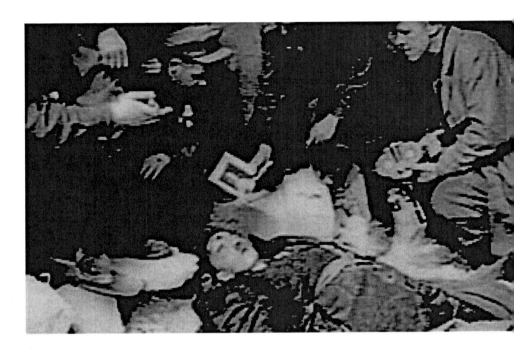

Russian officers examining the body of Gustave Weber (aka Gustav Weller), Hitler's double, Doppelanger in German. The double was shot in the head by either Martin Bormann himself or one of his SS thugs.

---

**Zarah Leander:**
Zarah Leander, Adolf Hitler's friend and favorite singer, told me verbatim, "Yes, Adolf Hitler had doubles, and Eva Braun had her double too, no question about it."

\*\*\*    \*\*\*    \*\*\*

Gustave Weber impersonating Adolf Hitler in honoring the Hitler Youth for heroic deeds in the defense of Berlin.

In a 1945 secret memo, General William Donovan, then head of the OSS, mentioned the existence of two possible doubles of Hitler.

Those two doubles were in fact carefully selected and trained by Josef Goebbels, back in 1944. The doubles received an extensive training on diction and Hitler's mannerism.

Worth mentioning here that General Donovan, then, head of the OSS (Office of Strategic Services), which functioned as the first US intelligence and counter-espionage agency (Precursor of the CIA) did not know much about Adolf Hitler.

In fact, General Donovan met Hitler in person at Berchtesgaden, and spent an "interesting evening" with Hitler in his private room at the "Pension Moritz", and had no clues who Adolf Hitler was, but one year later, he said publicly, "I did not recognize him, I did not know who he (Hitler) was, but surely he had a strong presence and was a fascinating talker."

General William Donovan, head of the OSS.

In October 1944, The FFL and the French Resistance in Lyon received information from one of their spies operating in Berlin, a French-Polish woman (Code-name Justine; real name Eva Kawalkowski) containing a reference made to a Hitler's double, who was chosen by Josef Goebbels, and was trained by a German cinema director from UFA. This was confirmed to me by Jean Gabin.

Jean Gabin in the center.

On March 13, 1939, Newsweek magazine published an article on Hitler's double (s).

Hitler without his mustaches.
What do you think?

In 1971, Simone Signoret told me that she learned from Marlene Dietrich while she was in Paris in the company of Jean Gabin that a minor actress from Berlin was chosen by Josef Goebbels to impersonate Eva Braun; she knew who she was but would not give her name to Simone.

Dietrich also told Simone that 2 doubles for Hitler were chosen by Josef Goebbels and were trained by a movie director from Düsseldorf. Marlene Dietrich reported this to FBI office in Los Angeles, despite the fact that she hated J. Edgar Hoover, then Director of the FBI who compiled an enormous file on her life, activities, friends, and especially on her lover, French actor Jean Gabin.

Zarah Leander told me verbatim, "Yes, Hitler had doubles, and Eva Braun had her double, no question about it. But I don't think Eva's double was a success. Geobbels changed his mind about her (Eva's Braun), despite the fact that she looked exactly like Eva Braun. Why? I don't know..."

**Hitler's four identified doubles.**

Hitler had four identified doubles according to hearsay, rumors, and articles in the Russian newspapers, whistleblowers, and finally quasi official military reports. Those doubles were:

1-Gustav Weber, aka Gustav Weller (Unknown figure)
2-Andreas Kronstadt (An actor)
3-Julius Schreck.
Hitler's driver who died in 1936 in a traffic accident
4-Heinrich Bergner.

Heinrich Bergner.

According to Time magazine, Heinrich Bergner was Hitler's double. Bergner was killed in July, 1944 by a bomb which exploded under Hitler's table, during Valkery's attempt to kill Hitler.

\*\*\* \*\*\* \*\*\*

Second from left, Heinrich Bergner. Hitler in the center.
See below.

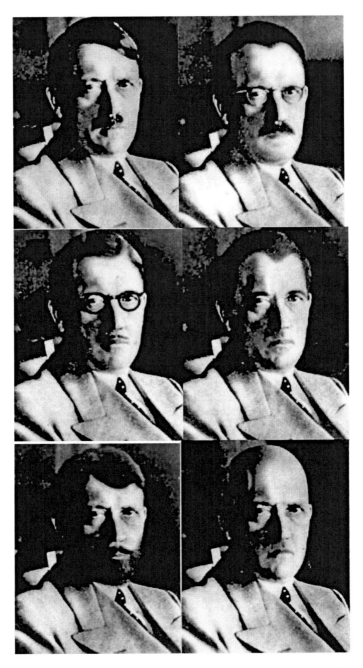

Six photos of Adolf Hitler found in the United States National Archives. Fearing that Hitler would/could escape from Germany, General Donovan, then Head of the OSS (Office of Strategic Services) commissioned Eddie Senz to create various possible portraits of Hitler, in case he disguised himself and/or to project how he might look like "throughout the ages."

**Lenni Riefenstahl:**
Leni behind the camera shooting "Triumph des Willens".

In an interview with Lenni Riefenstahl, she told me, "Hitler escaped!"

**SS Gruppenfuhrer Hans Baur:**
Hitler's personal pilot, Hans Baur told his Russian interrogators: "Adolf Hitler, Eva Braun and General Hans Fegelein escaped aboard a Ju 52."

**El Tiempo,** Colombia, 20th June 1948: "Hitler had escaped by submarine to South America."

**Los Angeles Times,** April 27, 1945: "Nazis Flying to Spanish Island."

Photo, left: Dr. Otto Schumann.

**Dr. Winfried Otto Schumann:**
In the early sixties, Dr. Otto Schumann, Professor at the Munich Technical University, told Hanna Reitsch that Hitler escaped on a supersonic-anti gravity "Vrill" he built himself using a mind-bending "Metal-Alloy Technology" unknown to scientists. This craft was called "RFC-2".

The RFC-2 was one of the two small crafts, designed by Maria Orsic, and developed by Dr. Schumann and four engineers.
It was an elegant craft with a shiny metallic surface, made from an unknown alloy; it was this kind of alloy the Russians were extremely interested in, because we know that Stalin's NKVD discussed with Dr. Eugene Sänger how such an alloy could be obtained.

101

**The origin of the name of god and his true identity.
Synopsis and Translation of the Phoenician, Ugaritic,
Canaanite, Sumerian, Akkadian, and Assyrian Tablets.**

The name of God "Yahweh", his attributes and extraordinary
(Supernatural) powers and deeds were borrowed from pagans'
gods; gods the Israelites worshiped before they "created" their
own god "Yahweh", who centuries later, became the God of the
Christians and the Muslims. So is it fair and logical to assume
that we are worshiping a "Pagans' God" or more precisely an
amalgam of mythical gods? You bet!
And this is exactly, the delicate, fragile and controversial topic we
will be exploring, discussing and explaining in this treatise. If you
are fanatically religious and you believe every word in the Bible,
and all the stories rabbis, sheiks, Imams, bishops and priests tell
you, then, do not read this treatise, because it could disturb you,

and lead you to believe that it was written to discredit your faith and your beliefs in the Jewish Bible, the Torah, Talmud, the Christian Bible (New Testament), Jesus, the Christian Church, the Koran, and the Prophets. And this is not the case at all.

The conclusions are based upon linguistic, historical, geographical, and archaeological facts and irrefutable findings, scrolls and inscriptions written centuries before any organized religion was established on Earth, and the word "GOD" was ever pronounced by or known to mankind.

Vital and most important questions we must address and answer:

a-God's true origin.
b-Where did he come from?
c-What is his real name?
d-How and why did Abraham, Moses, early believers, tribes, scribes, prophets, and others unintentionally or willingly change and/or misinterpret God's name or names?
e-How many names God had at the time, Abraham, Moses, and other prophets met him?
f-In what original language, his name was written?
What and how it was written?
And how it was translated in Greek, Latin, French, English, Spanish, etc.?
g-How did God himself pronounce his name?
h-Who heard God first?
i-When and where did the term or word "God" appear the first time in the history of humanity?
And what did it mean at that time; the very first time it was pronounced, used, and later put in writing?
Did the meaning change? No? Yes? Why?
j-Any relation to the Anunnaki, the Ancient Gods, the Sumerians, the Phoenicians, the extraterrestrials?


From the content:
• The real name of God.
• Allah's terminology.
• Yahweh was a common Phoenician name.
• The Phoenician source.
• The Phoenician words "Yehaw", "Yehi", "Yaw", and "Yeuo" are

the origin of the Hebrew words "Yah", "Yahu", and "Yahweh".
• Israelites bore the name of the Phoenician god Baal.
• Appearances of the word Yahweh outside and before the Bible was written (To name a few).
• The origins of Yahwehism.
• Phoenicia was the original source for the Hebrew Yahweh's imagery in the Bible and the "Cherubim Throne".
• Yahweh-Elohim and the Phoenician-Ugaritic Bull-Gods and the golden calves.
• Yahweh, and Ea/Enki create a spring in the Garden of Eden.
• Yahweh fighting the Dragon.
• "The Most High" epithet.
• On Monotheism.
• Epilogue: Quotes from leading scholars, and authors.

**How the Babylonian Story of the Flood Became the Story of the Great Deluge in the Bible. And How Utnapishtim Became Noah**

———————————————————

## THESAURUS AND LEXICON OF SIMILAR WORDS AND SYNONYMS IN 21 DEAD AND ANCIENT LANGUAGES AND DIALECTS.

From a set of 20 volumes. Thesaurus & lexicon of similar words and synonyms in 21 dead & ancient languages and dialects. Akkadian, Arabic, Aramaic, Assyrian, Urdu, Azerbaijani-Azeri, Babylonian, Canaanite, Chaldean, Essenic, Farsi, Ugaritic, Syriac, Hebrew, Mandaic, Nazorean, Phoenician, Turkish, Sumerian, Swadaya, and Turoyo.
The world's 1st dictionary/thesaurus/lexicon of its kind! A gem. A literary treasure! Written by the world's most prolific linguist who authored 21 dictionaries of dead and ancient languages known to mankind.

Published by
TIMES SQUARE PRESS
New York, Berlin

Printed in the
United States of America and Germany
August 2014

Lightning Source UK Ltd.
Milton Keynes UK
UKOW02f2126240716

279123UK00001B/25/P